You will Love this Book!

This is a book of details ... Details in keeping a relationship fresh and fun. It clarifies the Growth factor in everyone, and still be able to walk together in and on a productive journey. This book will help keep you mindful of making sweet memories even in at difficult times.

This Book is a great tool to help in the early stages of a young marriage and developing relationship.

If you follow these simple but easy principles, you will be ahead of the imposters that are surely lurking to disrupt and divide.

Norman Lynch is a Life Lecturer. A Bible Teacher (40 yrs.) who knows about the Bible. Motivational Speaker/ Family Game Producer.

Love Secrets after the Ceremony

Seven Principles of Growth in Maintaining Love

... And Exercises ...

Norman C. Lynch

Copywrite information

Author ... Norman C. Lynch

Finished ... April 25, 2021

Houston Texas

Acknowledgements

I am grateful to my Lovely Wife, our families and to my world of Friends who inspired me in any way.

Thank You

Thank You very much!

Content

Introduction

Understanding an individual is more than observing and learning their physical living habits; each of us (and particularly Black people) live and operate our life from three stages, that would be from a physical, intellectual, and spiritual platform.

We certainly get to know the physical by attraction and observation over time, while we learn the intellectual level of an individual by the frequency of communication and subject matter. The greatest understanding of another comes when receiving the seeds of wisdom, which flow from the spirit. We do not really know another until the spirits of the two have communed; When the experiences that made the most impressive impact in the spirit of one is shared with another, be it inspiring or revealing; it is then we can say we are getting to know them, or we *know them*. Association and time enrich this knowledge.

Marriage is like that. It is almost like the trust level, it is like an equation; the testing over time which makes for Trust, and it is Association over time which makes for Knowledge. Each of these are guided by and measured by the ability to *sensibly communicate!*

If we gave ourselves the luxury of knowing at least some of the fundamental issues abiding in, and sometimes deeply in the spirit of another; an understanding could come sooner and understanding has a friend called peace, which is pleasant to have around.

We must keep in mind that intellectual issues are not the same as spiritual issues. We can solve intellectual issues with logic and reason, although Spiritual issues have both, it is a deeper and higher degree of understanding that goes into the spiritual things, and yet the answer can come from a higher source.

Chapter One

Maintaining Focus

Life, Looks and Love

In this chapter look with me at the focus of our *life*, our *looks*, and the quality of *love* that we give to others, and particularly to those who are in the same household and family.

Life, real life brings liberty, labor and lessons. Life's opportunities are given by God, or from the favor of the Universe. It is an everyday opportunity to experience HIs Grace when we are given another chance at life. We are blessed daily with a fresh start.

We must keep in mind that everyone grows in some way whether we realize the change. People grow at different speeds, with different passions, and with a different degree of passion, and passions directed in many directions. One may begin to grow in certain areas faster than in others. The Grace of God has given us the freedom to Grow. It is the *edifying* of *the Spirit,* which abides in us.

Life has a way of changing on us, whether we approve or not. A song writer wrote *"Time is filled with swift transitions"* You might say our vision and views of life may not always turn out the way we had hoped. When we are young, there is something about our thinking that says to us "everyone else will get old, but not me" We think we will always be as strong and as swift as we were when young; however, there will come a day when something happens that brings the right understanding to our focus.

When we get married, life does the same thing as far as change is concerned, and unless we are aware of change and growth, Life seems to have doors waiting to allow intruders to enter our life.

Life has challenges, intellectual challenges, emotional and physical challenges. It is crucial that we understand that when a challenge come our way, we are to respond to it in the most calm and smooth way possible. The level of our maturity will help and determine how we respond.   That is why we should be aware of growth. It will help us emotionally as we go thru our challenges. Our emotions are tied up with our physical and certainly our trichotomous make up includes our intellect as well. (Body, soul, and spirit) Our intellect increases with knowledge, while our emotions change in degrees and interest; while we may be quit found of some things when young, our interest can change as we mature, including the taste for certain foods. When we learn new things, our interest can switch from one thing to something close or totally different. The intellect and emotions are influenced by outside elements which can be positive or negative. When two people communicate concerning the changes that are occurring, it helps bring in some calmness, and a greater degree of understanding *and* fellowship.

The intellectual changes that occur in the mind can cause our philosophy about life's issues to move in a different direction but, the mind will always hold the old thinking and the old knowledge at bay. There may have been an appreciation of the old to a high degree, but the growth in understanding, the decrease in passion to continue on the level once enjoyed in days gone by no longer holds true. I witnessed an older couple sitting together in the lobby of a hospital waiting as I was to get an x ray; a "finely built" and attractive young lady walked by; and as she did the old lady says to him, *"Now that is the kind you use to like"* they both smiled as he received the supposedly true statement from her. It appeared to me that communication was well and alive between them, *especially if they were husband and wife.* Recognizing past passions are a natural thing in the mind but, past physical passion will be replaced or altered by more mature ones with time. Maturity can increase or decrease many elements of life over time.

The changes that take place with and in the body are slow and sure. The care we give our body can prolong the inevitable and cushion the process.

And so, we have considered the fact of changes in Life, the Looks that attract. Now Love is the constant fabric in which we wrap this relationship journey. It is the vessel that need constant caring and maintenance. We want our relationship to be productive, fun, healthy in every way; as well as looking good. We will discuss in other chapters. Our focus is always on the road of keeping the Love safe from intruders; and rich enough *not* to become broken by selfish uncaring acts or demands.

Notes:

Projects

This is the Introduction to your Exercises. There are seven of them.

This book is to be completed when you have made an honest effort to complete each suggested project.

Each project has been thought out to accomplish ... closeness ... Insight ... Appreciation, and more. I will name them here. If you and yours are reading this book together, the assignments can easily be scheduled. They are to be done Ideally, after each chapter; if this is not possible, do what you can, but the completion of the book is when each project has been tackled.

1. Draw a picture   2. Have Fun

3. Competition 4. Accomplishment

5. Conscious   6. Sharing in the N

7. Review the A factor words

Project No. One ... Draw

Choose one of the scenes, or as many as you like. You will save these pictures to share with new members of the family, and friends to see.

You will take the time to use color, crayons, or color pencils.

1. Draw a picture of the neighborhood you grew up in.
2. Draw a room where you are living.
3. Draw a decorated buffet Dinner.
4. Draw an abstract from your spirit.
5. Draw a picture that shows relaxation.

6. Draw a picture that shows Family
7. Draw a picture of Love.

Chapter Two

Change, Adjustments and Love

There are only a few things in life that will not change, but, for most, you can count on change. Change is inevitable, it has a friend called Time. We can do nothing to stop change; but we can adjust to change as it comes around. Understanding this fact ... (did I say fact?) is not too difficult to mentally understand and grasp; however, emotionally in some cases it can be so much easier to say than to experience the journey of certain changes.

The word is called Adjustment. Adjustment is really one of several forms of change. The adjustment is the one form of change that we, the person must do to accept or reject whatever change that might come our way; because change is a constant factor, adjustments will be the same whether subtle or sudden.

There are simple changes, such as the time of an appointment or the place of an event which you may or may not have been the one to order the change; but, if you are part of the program, you as well as others must adjust your actions to correlate with the group. Whatever the level of the change, remember to stay focus on the important thing, the program.

Change comes through modifications and revisions; here, we adjust through our thinking. The pants are too long, and the jacket is too big. Although this is a reference to clothing, the principle of alterations can be made considering beauty, comfort, and safety. Our adjustment would be our judgement to what degree is best. The change of variations or a switch from one to more than one; that is, how many times, and which one or how many do we need? The change for correction can be difficult to receive unless obviously better, which would make the adjustment easier to accept; the only other challenge would be the effort needed to make the correction.

When we adjust for the benefit of the relationship, it huddles under the Love factor.

Change and turbulence; they do not need to partner. If change is inevitable, (unless it is danger or the threat of it), it would be wise to adjust to the change without turbulence. When we resist change or murmur about the adjustments, that can cause unnecessary turbulence; like anger, or regret, it opens the door for more imposters such as these.

Notes:

Project No. Two

This project is easy and fun. All I want you to do is find an air hockey table and *play at least three games together.*

Watch the reactions of each other, especially when you win.

You can find them in the lobby of a theatre.

Think about the games afterward, and how you felt while you were playing.

Compliment each other on the win games.

Chapter Three

New Establishment and Love

Never in the history of mankind has this experience been. This is the only wedding ceremony that took place at the time and place and with the uniqueness of which the two of you have brought into the Universe. Feel good about that. This is a new establishment! The passion that brought this unification was, and still is as diverse in mixture as that of every lovely cosmic snow-flack.

The challenge of days to come is to build upon whatever your foundation may be; that is one, and the next is, while building upon the foundation of your uniqueness, you must also strive to maintain and increase the growth of your Love.

Let us look at what is considered an establishment. We already know that marriage is the greatest institution on the planet; and so, we are not surprised why the evil one seeks to destroy the Family above everything else, and especially that of the Blackman. An establishment can be considered in several ways. When we think of an establishment; we know that there must be a formation as to how and from where you operate; there is also the organizational part of an establishment, that is how the two of you will organize your life together; here is a growth factor, because more than an establishment, it becomes an organism, capable of producing more of its kind. Establishments must be creative to promote goals and bring comfort and pleasure to your lives.

Behind the many changes and adjustments, we must know that this is a new establishment. It is different from your parents and different from their parents as much as you may be influenced by them, and with the inclination to copy some of the principles, which may be great; we must keep in mind that the two of you are building something incredibly unique. You will use the wonderful lesson from your parents; if that is the case, but you are pulling together the best from each past and from several influences. You are a product of your past and what you have gathered at this junction of your life is an end and a new beginning.

Your parents and siblings, friends and others who have known you are watching. They may not be conscious of you enough to write notes and keep records, but you can be assured they will get the news of your failures and successes; but even if they do not, you are displaying your Spirit's growth to the Universe to which you are accountable, and you are building something new with the strength of which you both contribute.

Rules that you establish are the rules of your house that the two of you must agree, even if it is much different from your past.

The best of you both has come together, and so the ideal is to establish an organization, an organism greater than your parents, some reflection but wiser in many segments of life. Certainly, you want to make them proud to know they did a good job in bringing you to this point in life, but not at the expense of not being and becoming who you really are meant to be.

It is an establishment of Love, and everything done, and every conversation must be drawn from the bowl of love; and one of the deepest elements from that bowl is Kindness, Caring and unselfishness, forgiving and giving; and so much more. You have become a Showcase of Love in your lifestyle branding your name and presence.

Like the other principles discussed in the paper, the highest degree possible of Love must be maintained, while at the same time growing in your Spirit through the Universe.

Meetings bring possibility. And that of fellowship, and of a greater understanding when communion, and conversation is practiced.

Notes:

Project No. Three

This Project is almost a continuation of the have fun project because it to is a fun game except it is also a mind game.

I want you to play a table game that neither of you have played before.

It must be a game that requires strategy to win.

Note: I have a list of games that are available but not yet on the market or they are new to the market, which means there is a great chance neither of you have played.

See index for list of games.

Chapter Four

The Owners Unselfish Planning of meetings.

Oh my!!! What a great idea just came to you; It makes so much sense to get involved or to make arrangement to purchase thru our good credit. ... Humm.

Hold it! ... and hold on a minute! I know you have the ability; but you must first get full authority from your partner before you make a significant transaction. Whatever level of significance you are on financially, is one of the major considerations before acting alone. Some activities warrant a discussion before closing. We plan meetings to consider reasons to spend and spend now or not to spend at all depending on the outcome of the factors of discussion.

There are many factors to consider before a major purchase; but there are at least three basic factors to consider. The first consideration might be do you really need it, and that need could be for anything, another factor could be, whether you would use it on a regular basis or would it be an impulsive act based on the excitement of the moment without the consideration of a long-term need, comfort, or passion; and then there is the factor of affordability. Does the money you have to make the purchase now already have a designated assignment?

Conversations and plans should flow through daily communications regarding the level of solo buying that would include the household budget. The understanding of financial goals and the spending freedom limits are crucial for the survival of financial growth.

These "*walking together*" meetings can be informal and fun. There will always be a formal meeting between the two of you; but the formal settings are whatever is designed by the two of you. Sitting at a table while eating, taking a walk together, sitting on a park bench, taking a drive to take in the scenery, the meeting may be formal, but the format can be of your choosing. Just have the meetings.

Meetings bring possibilities. Meetings bring greater fellowship, and greater understanding when we practice spiritual intimacy and good conversation. I can assure you that the number one problem in relationships is the scarcity of good Communication.

Notes:

Project No. ...Four

You will love this project! ... I think. It is a challenging one, for you will be working on it together.

I need you to buy construction art paper, and together make seven boxes with a different color.

Each box must be able to fit into the next. You can start with the smaller or the largest.

Take careful time because you will save the project to show and to remember.

Chapter Five

Expansions, More Adjustments, and Challenges

On the journey of Love, Expansions will come; some by your efforts and some will intrude. Whenever a change or challenge come across, there is always an adjustment however small or large.

Just when things seem to be under control, life presents another challenge. We are growing, we will need to expand the business or buy a larger house for the Children. Time goes by so swiftly, and always brings with it, Change.

There is a statement which says when facing a venture "Hope for the best, but prepare for the worst" ... well, if we were to consider the building of our marriage institute, much of the unfolding would have been considered in the planning meetings; so, we plan for challenges and changes. They are the sure issues of life.

Meetings should have a good balance in the agendas. I may not have to mention these, but to make sure, here are at least three things which should always be an underlined consciousness. The original vision and the anticipation, the operating skills and the expectations, and the jubilation for hitting a milestone goal.

Celebrating successes and planning on more. When accomplishments are met, adjustments are easy to understand; the adjusting activity could be having more things to do and a greater responsibility.

When it comes to expansions; it can apply to your conversations as far as subject matter. If you attend college, you will be introduced to more knowledge about more subjects, and so your conversations will expand; that is a good reason to become a life learner even if you do not attend college. You both will grow; the desire is to be able to grow together but not necessary in the same direction; however, it is possible to communicate on a higher level when you include at least an interest in your partner's interest. Having the same interest when you meet is crucial in having a great start, but as you both grow in the direction of your life's path, it is great to be able to communicate with each other on the level of your growth. This can help with the danger of relating to someone else more than that with your partner. You can certainly relate to others, for life will bring that around but you do not want to leave your partner out in the cold when you have a passion to discuss something of interest. Just to make sure; Interest, (things you are interested in) along with Attraction and emotions (things that light your fire) and things you both enjoy are the basic ingredients for the starting of a strong relationship.

Expansions can come in many different forms, starting at the waistline, some subtle, some sudden, but you can be sure, they are coming, and even the accumulation of things is a type of expansion; get ready to deal with these common events of life.

Notes:

Project No. ... Five

Conscious

This Project is to help you become more aware of yourself inwardly, and to be able to proclaim it to your mate.

You must get your personal attention by looking yourself in the eye through the mirror. You must look deeply in your own eyes and tell yourself how valuable you are to this generation and to your family. Tell yourself or remind yourself what a wonderful person you are, tell you about your Kindness, about your brilliance, and about the beauty the Universe and your Ancestors caused you to be born in, and ask yourself ...

Are you reaching to live your Best self?

You must do this when you are alone and able to focus.

That is, It!

Chapter Six

The richness of carving great Memories

Time can bring great memories. It might not be discussed often, but time also brings closeness and a greater understanding. Time can lock in idiosyncrasies to which we take for granted daily, but when we think of the other person, many of these unfocused activities come to mind. The richness is to put color to these minor movements by compliments.

These seemingly insignificant and idiosyncratic activities make up a great percentage of life's richness, into which we are growing; for they are a constant, seldom changing, but recognized as part of the physical identity of that person, and more, for there are other attitudes and verbal statements which are an expression of inner beauty, the moves, and the way they move, and at the rhythm in which they move is the uniqueness each of you possess. It depends on the longevity of the relationship as to how in depth the revelations can go.

"I did not know you had that in you," or "I did not know they had that in them." I know you have heard those words before, even from your own tongue. Those relationships are not in depth, either not awfully close or a short time acquaintance.

That does not mean the relationship is bad, it just has not had time to gather, and fully understand Life's Spiritual and Emotional levels at this junction. It takes time. Time brings about familiarity and knowledge. "I knew you could do it;" I have known you long enough to know that you are capable.

Relationships grows, one way or the other. That is why it is so important to communicate on a regular basis; that means as much as possible. It means as soon as possible when things are going ruff after an offensive act. We must be willing to listen, we must be willing to forgive, and we must be quick to admit error on our part if it is so.

These are life's classroom assignments and test. From this window, we are making memories that will help make it easier to check the records of our life. We are striving to make memories that are pleasant. We are also striving to be able to look back at our production and the progress of our growth; ... and so then we can say things like "We did it!" ... Can you believe we accomplished that!" ... Do you remember the Joy we had"! ... I'll never forget the trill and feeling of accomplishment!" and many others.

We must train our mind to store the nuggets of joy, and each piece of life's puzzle as we place them together while we live them, creating a Grand Gallery of Memories like acts of Arts and miniseries movies which we have displayed for the world, and for our Private Masterpieces. Memories! The reminiscing of days gone by ... recalling the circumstances .... Visiting old thoughts and holding on to past logic which brought about the inspiration to continue ...mentally reliving the feelings of victory ... pleasure, and ... the sense of accomplishments.

These days are the artful days in which we paint our pictures ... mold our clay ... and decorate the walls of the memory galleries to come. We do not want to walk through the halls of our future memory lane and have no inspiring memories on the walls to glare and stare with soothing reminiscences.

When we acknowledge different changes, natural or made; the recipient appreciates the notice; depending on how it was made. The new change could be something wanted or dreaded, but to recognize it in a loving and caring way can bring an inner strength to accept the change. It is almost like recognizing a new person, or the new person one has become.

This chapter, for the most part will be realized and understood as maturity sets in. (*You can smile right here)*

Notes

Project No. ... Six

In the Nude

Now you must get with your spouse and talk to them about the same. You must listen to their acknowledgement about them.

Ask Questions and give genuine compliments.

Keep everything positive and encouraging.

Have fun and be Inspiring.

This session should last at least 30 minutes.

Yes, In the nude without touching.

Chapter Seven

The A Factors

There are always factors, some may seem insignificant while others can prove to be crucial, depending on the issues and opinions. I like to use what I call the A factors. I suppose I could makeup what is called the ABC factors, but you may be a little familiar with a few of these As. Either way when using these factors in working a relationship, *(did I say working a relationship)* there is a good chance they will help bring an increase in understanding, and an appreciation for the ostensibly insignificant.

Let us present them in a synoptic form lest I bore you. There is no right or wrong order, but we will start with what may be called, fundamentals.

A great place to start the A's is to *Assemble:* we must come together obviously sometimes, and as often as possible. This word has friends like ... Build ... Gather ... Construct ... and more. Each of these words are used in the growth of any progressive relationship, and even for a business. It means more than coming together. When we assemble, the subjects are understood better, for there are fewer distractions if any.

Some conversations should be close enough to see the facial expression, and to be able to read the unspoken message which travels from *spirit to spirit* through the clairvoyancy of the eyes. Coming together has its benefits; Not only is there less chance of misunderstanding, but a better chance of coming to a genuine agreement, once all known logic and reason has been explored.

The Assembly says something good about each of you; at any time in the relationship that time is set apart or a schedule is rearranged to meet, says "I care enough to stop what I am doing to meet with you," You are that much important to me.

Another A is *Attention*. We must give attention to each other. It is not enough to be there physically, but to be focused and ready to verbally intercourse. Listening includes body language as well as your attendance. It is also a probing into the intentions of the speaker, if necessary.

Eye contact is good in many dialogues, however; it may be better to stare at an object with all other body languishes on point, if staring in the eyes of someone very physically attractive will cause your mind to wonder. If we are not careful ... the message or the conversation can be lost in the mixture of wondering thoughts.

We can get a clearer understanding, by asking questions. The simple act of giving attention can help us develop the art of communication. I will say this, *"good listening is slowing down your mind's multitasking, and focusing in on the developing message."* Mental or mind Busyness can cause that; the *"Art of Focus "*to be highly challenging, but it is possible, and worth it.

The next A for consideration is

Attractiveness and becoming more Attractive. An all-around appearance, it is the emotional, body languish, and charm which allures, even your spouse. Being Attractive is so much more than what you put on. It is more in how you wear them, and who is wearing them; (Did I say Who? ... I am not talking about lending out your clothes. It is *Which of YOU* will come to the meeting.

Perfect lined makeup or an affluent suit does not guarantee attractiveness. Attitudes, words, and facial expressions can cause physical beauty to appear as a turnoff, and you may wonder why you are suddenly alone, or why the conversation becomes silent for most of the remaining time together.

We must be attitude Attractive, in everything we do and everywhere we go we have an attitude consciousness, and it shows; if not, we are hiding the real thoughts which may not be altogether healthy. Verbal words are not always necessary, many times the attitude says it all, and sometimes, it is all that need be said. It is the beauty within, the inner man has the real message, and always wants to come out. We must work on keeping him inspired. ... avoiding negative input, looking for opportunities for genuine compliments, even if they are only thoughts without speaking them. This kind of attitude becomes attractive. People love it when you are around because they will begin to feel word safe around you. *Laughter and Inspirational statements are attractive*, even in serious settings.

Total Attractiveness can even cause others to feel good being around you.

We come now to a different mindset, if you will, Lets think in terms of how we view ... how we feel ... and how we value the efforts of our spouse. (Him and Her) The words are our Appreciation, Admiration, and the possibility of Adoration.

Appreciation is usually associated with effort and intent. It can be for the way things are done or what was conveyed in a statement or stand. It can be in that how a sensitive situation was handled. It can be the ability to pay attention to detail activity.

These words are so strongly associated that they have the same words of value in each definition.

If I had to say, I would suggest that we first learn to *Appreciate*, we can manage that by our thinking and by deciding to do so. When we notice the efforts made by others, their skill development, and the way they reach to accomplish their goals, the attitude toward life, and the way they strive to treat others with kindness; we can then begin to *Admire*. *Adoration*, I believe comes with time and testing.

I have looked up the basic words for each so that you can study these on your own. I want you to work on each of these to make them part of your personal character and use the positive form almost without thinking.

Learn to Appreciate ... Love and Admire ... Grow to Adoration.

Appreciation: Gratitude ... Pleasure ... Understanding ... Gratefulness ... Admiration.

Admiration: ... Awe ... Respect ... Esteem ... Wonder ... Appreciation

Adoration: ... Adulation ... Admiration ... Devotion ... Veneration ... Reverence

Approachable

When a person is somewhat laid back and easy going, it becomes easier to come to them with an idea or a suggestion. We must work on that demeaner. It does not mean anything goes or to allow people to take advantage of you. It gives a greater appeal for people to be honest and willing to give and ask advice when needed and wanted. (do be careful giving advise unsolicited) Friendliness increases the joy of good conversation.

Adaptable

The same principle here with Adaptable. It is having a flexible mode of communicating. To be in a different setting without complaining, but rather compliant is being adaptable. We can eat on the patio today, or in the living room for a change, and make it fun.

Notes

Project No. ... Seven

You may know that this Project is to review the A factors and study their meanings,

Talk about the other projects and the Book in general.

Have fun in this Growth
Incarnation!